C000016377

PLANTS IN POTS

F

FRANCES LINCOLN LIMITED
PUBLISHERS

PLANTS
IN
POTS

ANDI CLEVELY

PHOTOGRAPHY BY
MARK BOLTON

Frances Lincoln Ltd
4 Torriano Mews
Torriano Avenue
London NW5 2RZ
www.franceslincoln.com

Plants in Pots
Copyright © Frances Lincoln 2008
Text copyright © Andi Clevely 2008
Photographs copyright
© Mark Bolton 2008

First Frances Lincoln edition: 2008

Andi Clevely has asserted his right to
be identified as the author of this
work in accordance with the
Copyright, Designs and Patents Act
1988 (UK).

All rights reserved. No part of this
publication may be reproduced,
stored in a retrieval system or
transmitted in any form, or by any
means, electronic, mechanical,
photocopying, recording or otherwise,
without either permission in writing
from the publisher or a licence
permitting restricted copying. In the
United Kingdom such licences are
issued by the Copyright Licensing
Agency, Saffron House, 6–10 Kirby
Street, London, EC1N 8TS.

A catalogue record for this book is
available from the British Library.

ISBN 978-0-7112-2749-1

Printed and bound in Singapore

9 8 7 6 5 4 3 2 1

Containers can provide homes for a
wide range of occupants, from
complete miniature gardens (page 1),
to flowering wall finials (page 2), to
spring bulbs (right).

CONTENTS

INTRODUCTION

Origins

Growing plants in pots is one of the most rewarding kinds of gardening. Far from being second best to tending beds and borders, or a way of compensating if you live in an apartment or town house without any kind of conventional garden, it is a practical skill that recognizes and appreciates plants as individuals, singling each out from the crowd and proclaiming its unique qualities. As an extra dimension to conventional gardening, cultivation in containers offers a host of opportunities for displaying choice plants as special features, while for those with yards, roofs or balconies it is a triumphant and versatile solution to landlessness.

Despite its long pedigree (see page 10), container gardening is even sometimes cynically perceived as a fashion driven by a gardening trade keen to expand the use of bedding plants in hanging baskets or plastic planters. But any change in recent decades has been one

Clay pots are traditional containers for plants of all kinds. They are both utilitarian and unobtrusive, blending effortlessly with landscape elements like brick and gravel.

Trees are remarkable individuals and when grown in pots can lay claim to stardom. Citrus trees are traditional container aristocrats. Note their ground-level wedges for enhanced drainage.

of emphasis and availability, for gardeners have always grown plants in pots.

Early Greek and Roman accounts refer to medicinal herbs kept in reed baskets and 'casks filled with earth', while the classic description of Babylon's legendary Hanging Gardens suggests soaring tiers of balcony boxes and an elaborate system of 'engines supplying the gardens with water', perhaps an early version of the trickle irrigation used today to automate watering containers.

Emperors and aristocracy studded their manicured acres with stone urns, lead troughs and carpentered boxes as focal highlights and specialized habitats for rare plants. As part of their advanced training journeymen gardeners learned the arcane secrets of mixing special composts for these temperamental exotics, adding a dash of deer dung, brick dust or Peruvian guano depending on the species. Nothing less, it was thought, would do.

Widening the appeal

For all their ill-effects elsewhere, standardization and mass production drove the changes which extended container

Container garden through the ages

Ancient hieroglyphics record expeditions organized by an Egyptian queen to collect trees from neighbouring territories, and show the trees growing in deep baskets suspended from poles across the shoulders of slaves. At European palaces and stately homes in the sixteenth century citrus trees were grown in large wooden boxes housed every winter in the orangery, safe from frost. For centuries Japanese citizens have resolved land shortages by growing a range of plants, even lawns and hedges, in pots of various kinds. Today Cuban gardeners raise organic vegetables in old tyres filled with home-made compost and lined out on their flat roofs. And container cultivation has been suggested as a practical strategy for the future in regions where climate change renders traditional soil management difficult or impossible.

The sculptural eccentricity of some plants, such as cloud-pruned topiary (left) and the angular segmented fronds of many palms (right) are balanced by the calm restraint of capacious glazed jars.

gardening to everyone. In the 1930s soil scientists realized that the majority of plants would flourish happily in the same basic kind of compost, provided it satisfied certain crucial growth requirements.

The result was the standard range of John Innes soil-based composts. They were followed by a multi-purpose soil-less alternative, and between them these mixtures replaced the old esoteric concoctions, simplifying the potting process and giving many more gardeners an inexpensive and readily obtainable potting compost (or basic formulae for mixing their own), together with the confidence to try it.

A little afterwards, plastic began to replace clay, at first only for the everyday range of standard flowerpots in general greenhouse use, but later for making a host of sometimes very convincing replicas of traditional terracotta, stone, lead and timber containers.

Inspired by this ready supply of dependable composts and inexpensive pots, gardeners began to explore the available plant repertoire, a growing interest which in turn stimulated the seed and nursery trades to offer an ever-expanding range of plants that were suitable, even exclusively designed, for container culture.

With increasing numbers of people (more than three-quarters of the population in the UK, for example) living in urban areas where gardens are generally small or non-existent, gardeners face enormous challenges but equally numerous opportunities to use potted plants to embellish

One of the many advantages of growing plants in containers is their easy rearrangement for display, as here where a table-top collection adds an extra temporary tier to a patio corner.

an existing garden with extra detail or to create one where there is little or no soil. All the essential materials are there to satisfy the most ambitious schemes and dreams.

Plants as individuals

In many ways plants seem to matter more when they are growing in pots, perhaps because they claim (and usually receive) more personal attention. An old saying that the best fertilizer is the gardener's footsteps refers to the benefits of regularly walking round and inspecting the state of the garden, and this is especially true for container plants. They are almost totally dependent on you for their welfare: the volume of compost available to their roots is restricted, so routine watering and feeding are vital for success – much more so than in the open garden. This systematic attention ensures that any early signs of discontent or ailment are quickly spotted. It is also easier to maintain the well-being of an individual in a pot than a multitude in a border.

This applies particularly to plants with special needs. Pampered show auriculas and monstrous exhibition parsnips are often grown in containers, where conditions

are individually tailored and finely tuned to suit their exacting requirements. Whatever the prevailing conditions in the wider surroundings, you could plan a private world in a pot to create the ideal habitat for a lime-hating *Magnolia stellata*, sun-loving thymes and rosemaries in a tower of gritty compost, a colony of insectivorous bog plants in a nearly waterlogged bowl or a cluster of shy alpine soldanellas from scree slopes. You could even have them all in the same garden.

Because most containers are portable, you can also shift these plants around to ensure each gets the amount of sun or exposure it prefers, especially if the weather changes or a plant shows signs of distress – which is not a practical option with open garden plants. And when one of your charges starts flowering, you can move it centre-stage so that you can enjoy its performance and appreciate its individuality.

Looking after pots

The amount of time and space you can devote to container plants is inevitably finite, so there is no place for mediocre or lacklustre passengers: each must be a hand-picked star, with the character and performance to earn its board and keep.

Although growing plants in pots is a manageable and relatively low-maintenance kind of gardening, looking after them involves a certain amount of commitment. All plants are inherently self-sufficient and 'free-range', and removing one from its natural environment and confining it in a pot limits its ability to fend for itself. Instead you assume responsibility for watering and feeding, providing adequate rooting space for unhampered growth and ensuring protection from trouble.

These responsibilities are far from onerous (unless you are trying to grow an unsuitable plant in the wrong place) and can be easier than conventional gardening, especially for anyone who has difficulty working at ground level.

Watering is the most regular commitment, usually at a time when it is pleasant anyway to be outdoors – and containers can actually star in a drought, because they are easier to keep watered than the open ground. While watering you have the opportunity to give your plants a health check, perhaps deadhead fading blooms or rearrange the display if necessary. Most other duties are infrequent: just once annually in the case of repotting.

The rewards

In return you can have plants where otherwise none would grow, because pots are the simplest solution to the problem of gardening in a completely built environment, on balconies, patios and window sills, against walls and even on roofs. You can stage-manage displays and change them as often as you like, even for just a single evening alfresco. Plants that might sulk in your soil or cower from exposure to sun and wind become a realistic option when given personal care in a container.

Frost-tender citrus trees like this calamondin orange
(x *Citrofortunella microcarpa*) are classic container plants,
seasonally moved between summer sunshine and winter
protection indoors in a conservatory or a well-lit window.

And you can experiment with species, styles and
combinations that might be inappropriate or impossible
in the open garden. Suggestions could include:

- creating figurative or abstract topiary, transforming
  yew, box, rosemary or ivy into living sculpture to
  guard an entrance
- cloud-pruning a juniper planted in a crate topped
  with moss and stones for an oriental atmosphere
- growing asparagus, artichokes or cardoons in hand-
  made concrete boxes as dual-purpose crops and
  thickets of ornamental foliage
- introducing a hint of tropical exuberance with banana
  plants, trachycarpus, Japanese sago palms (*Cycas
  revoluta*) or just a vat full of giant *Gunnera manicata*
- draping a sunny wall with mixed trailing nasturtiums
  cascading from old paint tins suspended on hooks
- planting stark aeoniums or absurd opuntias as patio
  conversation pieces
- turning a half-barrel into a miniature oasis of reeds,
  rushes and glamorous water hyacinths
- sowing large pots with a designer mix of wildflowers
  to stand in the sun and attract butterflies into view.

The keys to success

Growing plants in pots is simple provided you follow a
few basic guidelines.

Pots (see Chapter 1) With the wealth of shapes,
genres and materials available it is important to use a
container that supplies the best growing conditions for
the plants you have chosen. Appearance, cost and
durability all need taking into account when buying.

Places (see Chapter 2) Using pots allows you to grow
plants where there is no ground or stage them in
strategic places around the garden. This means
thinking like a designer while bearing in mind the
cultural needs of your plants, which might have strong
preferences about aspect or exposure.

Plants (see Chapter 3) Given a favourable kind of
container and position, almost any plant, from a large
tree to a tiny alpine, can be grown. Choosing the most
appropriate candidate can be bewildering unless you
first decide exactly what you have in mind.

Practice (see Chapter 4) Adopting the best growing
method results in contented plants that grow and
perform well. Routine care for most is straightforward.

TYPES of CONTAINER

Almost anything capable of holding soil or compost, from a recycled string bag to an expensive majolica pot, can be used for growing a plant. Some kinds are more appropriate for particular purposes or plants than others, however, while beauty can be as important as utility where plants are to be staged as prime specimens in conspicuous places. Whatever their purpose or position all types of container must satisfy a few elementary criteria if they are to support vigorous and trouble-free plantlife.

Different recycled utensils can be used to house plants of varying habit. Trailing pelargoniums look well in ornate ice buckets (page 16); compact succulents fit nicely in tin cans (left) and robust rhubarb thrives in an old galvanized washtub (opposite).

numerous small holes at the bottom. Drill holes in the base of an undrained container or use it as a cachepot, an ornamental holder for a plain flowerpot, standing the inner pot on a few pebbles and checking it is not awash after heavy or prolonged rain.

WHAT EVERY GOOD POT NEEDS

An apparently limitless choice of containers at garden centres and potteries often makes selection a difficult decision. Manufacturers appreciate that appearances are important, and many gardeners amass patio containers with the same enthusiasm and discrimination as collectors of fine pottery or bone china. But aesthetic appeal is just one consideration, however compelling: from the point of view of a plant other factors are more crucial.

Drainage Containers for terrestrial plants need to drain surplus water efficiently if the compost is not to become waterlogged and threaten the plant's health. Clay and stone pots usually have one large central hole in the base, and bigger sizes may have several, evenly spaced and about 1cm (½in) in diameter. Plastic pots often have

Stability An outdoor container is likely to be exposed to wind or accidental knocks from passers-by, so a substantial base is advisable for stability; alternatively make sure there is enough room inside for a generous gravel drainage layer to add weight at the base (see page 88).

Balance this against the possible need to limit the loading on balconies or roof gardens. A tub 1.2m (4ft) wide and 1m (39in) deep, for example, might weigh 20kg (45lb) empty but when filled with 100 litres (22 gallons or 10 large bucketsful) of moist compost could weigh up to 200kg (nearly 4cwt).

Any container will obviously be much heavier and therefore more stable when filled with compost and plants, but remember that plants grow and can become top-heavy, which increases their wind-resistance, especially if they are kept in tall narrow containers.

Durability As well as wind, outdoor containers must withstand frost, rain and strong sunlight. For permanent planting it is important that the chosen materials are reasonably weatherproof and easy to maintain. Appearance can change after continuous weathering: some materials develop an attractive colour or patina, whereas others become dull or tarnished.

MATERIALS FOR POTS

Containers are made from a number of materials, some strictly functional and others more appealing. Personal taste will inevitably play a large part in your choice, but you need to balance this with their practical virtues. Natural materials usually look best in relaxed settings and some gardeners confine their collection to these, especially in high-profile positions. For massed displays more utilitarian pots will often suffice and cost less to buy.

Clay and terracotta Traditional and versatile, with an attractive finish even when old, worn and stained with lime-scale. A host of shapes, styles and sizes is available, although larger kinds can be very expensive. As these pots are porous, their contents can breathe but usually dry out faster than they would in other materials – for moisture-loving plants, line the sides of pots with polythene. Handle carefully to avoid breakage, especially in very cold weather (although repair is sometimes possible), and make sure

Wooden boxes make ideal and inexpensive seasonal homes for vegetables, bedding and annual herbs (below); perennials need more permanent accommodation in durable clay or metal containers (opposite).

permanent containers are guaranteed frost-proof. Ceramic pots are colourful, but as they are glazed they are not porous and are sometimes easily chipped; glazes can craze wildly in cold regions.

Plastic and fibreglass These are popular for lightweight and inexpensive containers, from plain flowerpots to moulded simulations of stone, lead and terracotta. Some heavy-duty imitations look convincing and weather well, and a wide range of colours is available, but cheaper kinds can become brittle and faded after a few seasons' exposure. Even when full these are usually easier to move than other materials. Plastic is a poor insulator against extreme heat and frost, but very resistant to drying out.

Wood A natural, durable and unobtrusive choice, with good insulation properties. Soft woods have low resistance to rot unless painted regularly with a plant-friendly preservative, but oak, cedar and chestnut do not need treatment. Wooden containers are available in a range of styles, from square planters and window boxes to coopered half-barrels and recycled tubs. Wood is the best material for DIY construction, but make sure new timber comes from a managed renewable source. Wickerwork baskets can be used if treated against rot and lined with plastic.

Aligned on a matching paved surface like cool sentinels, these tall stone containers would have an arresting presence by themselves, even without their caps of tightly packed foliage and flowers.

Stone Impressive and usually expensive, whether natural or reconstituted (cast terrazzo), and mainly used for simple troughs and sinks or classically ornate urns, although contemporary designs are also available. All provide good insulation and are attractive when weathered but can be extremely heavy to move. Concrete is the least costly 'stone' material, often used for plain shapes and simple designs, and can be unexpectedly good-looking.

Metal Stylish, robust and eye-catching, whether as traditional lead or iron cisterns or modern copper or stainless steel pots. Metal quickly conducts heat and cold, which can expose roots and compost to extreme temperature changes, but containers may be insulated with a plastic liner or used as a cachepot to hold a conventional inner pot. Large tin cans make excellent recycled pots, as do wire waste-paper baskets when lined with plastic (disguise the functional appearance of this by tucking bracken or conifer prunings between liner and mesh).

SHAPES AND STYLES

Many lovely container shapes and designs originally
evolved as practical solutions to the specific requirements
of different kinds of plants. For example, the extra tall pot
known as a long tom was designed for growing sweet
peas and similar deep-rooted plants, whereas half-pots,
pans and bowls are suitable for smaller, more modest
plants like crocuses, cyclamen and sempervivums, which
either do not require a deep root-run or positively resent
large volumes of stagnant soil around their roots. So
when buying a new container temper impulse with an
appreciation of the plants you would like to grow.

Tall slender containers like florists' buckets, land drains
and large jars suit trailing flowers and foliage plants, such
as nasturtiums, periwinkles and cascading petunias, as
well as those which like a deep cool rooting environment
– conifers and lilies, for example. Remember that plants
can be difficult to remove from containers that taper
towards the top. Shallow-rooting plants can be grown in
a conventional pot or pan nestled inside a tall container
such as a chimneypot or drainpipe.

Shallow pans and wide bowls are ideal for smaller
bulbs and cacti, mosses, short grasses and many
creeping or mat-forming plants like pennyroyal and thrift.
Alpines are traditionally grown in a gritty compost in a
shallow sink or trough no more than 15–20cm (6–8in)
deep, while bonsai trees need very little compost (but a
lot of attention) and are kept dwarf by the restriction of
their roots in special trays and pans often less than 5cm

Containers allow bulbs – whether hardy or as frost-shy as this Guernsey lily (*Nerine sarniensis*) – to be prominently displayed while flowering and then moved off-stage. Clay pots supply the free drainage most bulbs enjoy.

(2in) deep. These need conscientious watering, whereas cacti, succulents and some woody herbs can tolerate occasionally drying out.

Really spacious containers like tubs, half-barrels and the square wooden planters called Versailles boxes have the capacity to grow shrubs, soaring perennials, fruit and ornamental trees, often with an underplanting of other shorter plants like bedding and edging flowers.

Note the distinction between an informal, almost rustic container like a half-barrel, which is more suitable for a homely bedding or cottage garden combination of plants or for a small water garden, and more sophisticated designs like the Versailles box, which complements elegant topiary, aristocratic subjects like citrus, bay and palms, and fat clumps of bamboo or agapanthus. For the most satisfying effect, match style carefully to both setting and specimen: a plain modern container might suit blueberries grown for their fruit and autumn leaf tints (in lime-free compost), whereas a plain but shapely evergreen would flatter a lavishly decorated glazed urn.

POT SIZES

As a rule plants in small containers need more frequent watering and potting on, and it might seem sensible to use a larger pot straight away to save time and effort later. Slower-growing species can resent 'over-potting', however, and unoccupied compost soon loses its good condition. It is best to start very young plants in 9–13cm (3½–5in) pots. Keep these out of hot sun, packed in trays for stability

Anchoring pots

Expensive containers appeal to collectors and crooks alike. Heavier tanks, urns and planters are difficult to carry off, but smaller pots are easier to steal and in some neighbourhoods may need making fast in some way. While it is empty, lower a permanent pot via its drainage hole over a sturdy stake driven firmly into the ground, and then fill and pot as normal around this – make sure this doesn't impede drainage, though. Alternatively loop a chain through the base, round a short piece of metal rod lying inside the pot and then back to a ring set in the ground or a wall, and secure with a padlock.

outdoors, and water them regularly with a fine rose.

Many seasonal bedding plants such as salvias, petunias or impatiens can spend their whole lives in 10, 13 or 15cm (4, 5 or 6in) pots. To compose a massed display, these can be plunged to their rims in larger containers like tubs and window boxes filled with used compost or composted bark to stop the pots drying out quickly. As flowers fade, pots can be exchanged for younger specimens in bud or a different species to extend the display.

A wooden half-barrel offers the capacity and depth for a whole community of annuals, perennials and even deep-rooting lilies. Jack up tubs on feet or blocks to speed drainage and extend the container's life.

The minimum size of pot for a permanent plant is about 23cm (9in) in diameter and depth, and many species will need potting on into larger containers as they mature and expand. Fruiting and ornamental trees prefer a container at least 38–45cm (15–18in) across, but with annual repotting and pruning will remain in good condition at that size for many years.

Where a much larger container like a trough or barrel is used for bedding or similar shallow-rooted plants, you can reduce the weight and volume of compost by first filling up to half the depth with broken polystyrene plant trays without compromising growth; most rooting activity will occur in the upper 15–20cm (6–8in) of compost.

IMPROVISED CONTAINERS

With a little inventiveness, a host of discarded utensils and receptacles can be used for growing plants or as cachepots to disguise plainer inner pots.

Kitchenware and household bric-a-brac are fertile resources – a colander as a hanging basket, kettles and coal scuttles as pots, for example – while more industrial remnants are often easily adapted: drain sections, flue pipes, oil drums, paint tins and old car tyres turn into

Capacity

Instructions to 'fill the pot with compost' can be vague and unhelpful until experience allows you to estimate how much compost to buy (bear in mind that any left over gradually deteriorates in quality).

Compost is generally sold by the litre. Many larger pots are identified by their capacity (1 litre, 2 litre, 2½-litre, for example) but others are labelled according to diameter, and it may be a surprise to find that a 30cm (12in) pot takes as much as 15–17 litres of compost.

As a rough guide, expect a 9cm (3½in) pot to use about ¼ litre of compost, a 13cm (5in) pot 1 litre, and 15cm (6in) 2 litres. A 75-litre sack can fill approximately 320 x 8cm (3in), 80 x 13cm (5in) or 5 x 30cm (12in) pots, or about 24 standard seed trays.

effective containers for various kinds of plants. Strawberries will trail and fruit happily in guttering fixed (with a gentle slope for drainage) to a wall, while buckets and wooden crates can yield prolific crops of potatoes.

Any example must have adequate drainage holes or slots in the base, and it is a sound precaution to scour or brush off any rust and loose paint that might prove toxic to plants. Coat bare timber with preservative and paint iron or steel with a rust-proofing agent to extend its useful life (although rust can be an attractive finish in a naturalistic setting).

Old plastic containers such as stacking boxes and washing bowls can be given a facelift with one or two coats of exterior paint or may be concealed under a layer of hypertufa (see page 35) to give an impression of natural stone. Progressive weathering and disguise by trailing plants will soon soften a stark, industrial or uncompromising appearance.

HANGING BASKETS

Lifting plants off the ground adds an extra dimension to garden displays, decorating vertical surfaces with seasonal luxuriance and gaiety, and allows you to include trailers and lax edging plants in your choice of plants to grow. The most popular kind of raised container is the hanging basket, but other options include window boxes (see page 31), plastic flower pouches (see page 33) and individual flowerpots suspended from a wall in wire hangers or mounted on stands.

Decorating the façade of buildings with flowering plants in troughs and pots or boxes suspended on balcony railings adds colour and life to the built environment, helping to 'green' cities and improve a neighbourhood's ambience.

True hanging baskets have open sides and are made from galvanized or plastic-coated wire meshed into a hemisphere or from wooden slats arranged as a square box. This type is intended for planting all round to produce a ball of foliage and flowers, but needs a liner to prevent the compost from falling out and drying too fast. This liner can be made from moss (possibly raked from your lawn), plastic sheeting or treated cardboard, but the best materials are wool, fibre or plastic foam because they are more moisture-retentive and better insulators.

Solid-sided plastic, clay or fibre 'baskets' are really suspended pots or bowls. These do not need lining, and are sometimes fitted with an integral drip tray or reservoir to ease the watering routine. Most of these are planted up only at the top.

To extend the growing season, start baskets in mid-spring in a greenhouse or conservatory so that they are already flowering well when transferred outdoors after any frosts. As temperatures fall in autumn move them back indoors for a few extra weeks' display.

How to plant a basket

To relieve the need for frequent attention, use the largest size of basket available (about 35–45cm/14–18in diameter), fit a good liner and mix water-retaining gel into the compost.

- Steady the basket on a bucket or tall pot, fit the liner and centre a saucer inside to help retain water. Fill one-third of the depth with soil-less compost and firm gently.

- Space four or five young trailing plants or even smaller plug plants round the sides, pushing them through holes or slits in the liner so that their roots rest on the surface of the compost.

- Add more compost, firm with your fingers and insert another layer of plants. Cover these with compost almost to the rim and plant up the surface with upright plants in the centre and trailers round the rim.

- Water thoroughly and keep in a sheltered place for two or three weeks until the plants are growing well. Harden off tender species, gradually accustoming them to outdoor conditions, and move them permanently into position outdoors after the last frosts.

- To make a complete ball, fill and plant the sides of two identical baskets, cover one with a sheet of stiff card or plywood and invert it over the other basket. Slide the sheet out and 'stitch' the two rims together with strong wire. Suspend the ball at the seam.

WINDOW BOXES

Once the preserve of well-dressed country cottages and alpine chalets, window boxes have become a popular option for decorating the façade of any home, especially apartments without other gardening space. The range of plants grown has expanded too, from traditional trailing carnations or ivy-leaved pelargoniums to vibrant summer bedding displays, bulbs, evergreen climbers and dwarf conifers, and even herbs and vegetables.

A few simple precautions will help ensure success.

- A box can sit on the sill if the window does not open outwards; otherwise it must be supported below sill level. Remember that mature plants can seriously obscure your view and the amount of light entering the room, as well as possibly obstructing an opening window.

- For safety provide strong supports – side fixings for sill-level boxes together with wedges to level the floor, or brackets and screws at the back for boxes on the wall beneath the sill. A drip tray under the box will protect people living or passing below.

- For visual balance and symmetry a box extending the full width of the window or slightly more will look best, but you may need to adapt the size depending on access and the type of sill or window.

- Bought boxes are likely to be made from plastic or fibreglass (sometimes with an integral drip tray or reservoir), metal including replica lead or zinc, or wood. You can make your own from 2cm (3/4in) thick boards, treated if necessary with preservative.

A well-lit flight of steps is ideal for staging a tiered collection of red and white potted pelargoniums in full sun, each pot supplied with its own saucer to catch excess water draining from its base.

Plants for baskets

A huge and increasing range of flowers is available for seasonal basket displays.

- Most summer-flowering bedding plants are ideal for the top of baskets, including begonias, fuchsias, impatiens, pelargoniums and tagetes.

- Trailing plants to try include bidens, *Convolvulus sabatius*, desmodium, *Helichrysum petiolare*, ivy-leaved pelargoniums, trailing lobelia, scaevola, thunbergia and trailing petunias.

- For winter baskets: *Bellis perennis*, miniature cyclamen, glechoma, heathers, ivies, ornamental kale, winter-flowering pansies.

- For productive baskets: nasturtiums (edible flowers and seeds), New Zealand spinach, parsley, strawberries (perpetual 'Aromel' and alpine kinds), trailing tomatoes ('Gartenperle' and 'Tumbler').

Provided they are planted in a porous compost kept open with extra grit, succulents will grow happily in the smallest containers, like this aeonium in a 15cm (6in) pot mulched with pebbles or the sempervivum bubbling out of its clay sphere.

- Make sure there are adequate drainage holes every 10–15cm (4–6in) along the base. Fix the box in position before filling with broken crocks to cover the holes, followed by a 2.5cm (1in) lightweight drainage layer of polystyrene beads. Then fill with moist soil-less compost and water well to settle this in place.
- Instead of planting directly into the box, consider fitting inner boxes or baskets that can be planted up elsewhere and exchanged with others as the display fades. Alternatively you can plunge pot plants up to their rims into a matrix of vermiculite or composted bark, and replace these with a sequence of younger or more seasonal potted plants.

SPECIAL CONTAINERS

A number of variations on traditional containers have been developed, often for specific purposes.

Strawberry tower A tall plastic or terracotta pot or jar, perforated around the sides with holes or lipped pockets, each for holding a single strawberry plant. A tower can also be used for a collection of herbs, bulbs or flowering plants (more modest versions include crocus and parsley pots). It is filled gradually with compost and planted in stages in the same way as a hanging basket (see page 30). It is sometimes difficult to keep evenly watered, so add extra grit to the compost, or stand a section of drainpipe in the centre of the pot at planting time, fill this with grit, and when you have finished twist out the pipe to leave a porous core.

Growing bags Long, flat plastic bags filled with soil-less compost, popular for growing tomatoes and other summer vegetables. There is no reason why they cannot be used as annual beds for other vegetables, herbs or flowers, although the contents are not generous, and for top yields it is best to layer one on top of another with communicating holes cut out between the two to double the potential rooting depth. Disguise the often garish plastic by constructing a timber surround and then fill all round the bag with loose mulching material such as cocoa shells or bark (this will also help retain moisture). If you loosen and fortify their contents with a little general fertilizer, growing bags can often be used for a second season.

Flower pouches These are miniature growing bags studded with planting holes or pockets and intended for hanging vertically against a wall. Add water-retaining gel to the compost before filling. Pouches can be planted

A hanging container such as this deep basket makes a perfect safe haven for leafy vegetables like cutting lettuce, out of the reach of slugs but handy for harvesting for the table.

Every gardener is an artist at heart! Swirls of bright paint transform this unexceptional pot into a flamboyant example of *joie de vivre*, matched with an equally gaudy collection of anemones and ranunculus.

with the same trailing varieties recommended for hanging baskets, compact bedding plants like mimulus, impatiens or petunias, or edible crops such as parsley, summer savory, basil or leaf lettuce for cutting with scissors.

DECORATING CONTAINERS

Even when empty many pots are handsome works of craftsmanship without need of further embellishment. Others may look uninspiring, but there are a number of techniques for transforming plain, salvaged or recycled containers.

Paint Inexpensive plastic flowerpots can acquire character when painted with two or three coats of coloured limewash, left-over emulsion, tile or blackboard paint applied over an exterior primer. Metallic or crystalline paint gives plastic and clay a designer finish, special verdigris kits confer instant weathering and coloured preservatives can enhance bare wood.

Artificial ageing You can accelerate the weathering of concrete and plain stone surfaces by painting them with a runny mixture of natural yoghurt and manure stirred in water. This stains the surface and encourages the rapid establishment of mosses and lichen.

Hypertufa Glazed sinks, concrete containers, plastic troughs and even polystyrene boxes are easily transformed into imitation stone by coating them with

The cool aseptic finish and stark geometric lines of these aluminium and galvanized steel containers suit the industrial style of a contemporary home, and set off the flowing organic shapes of leaves and stems.

As eye-catching as many more lavish compositions, this restrained arrangement uses a limited palette – a satin-finished metal container, an immaculate green sphere and quietly neutral gravel – to echo a setting of neatly clipped box hedging. Together they create an atmosphere of calm and peace.

hypertufa, an artificial finish very like natural volcanic rock. Mix together 1 part cement and 2 parts sand (or use dry ready-mixed mortar), plus 2 parts crumbled soil-less compost, and add enough water to make a smooth workable mixture. Paint the container thickly with exterior grade PVA adhesive, and while this is still tacky spread a coat of hypertufa over the whole surface. For strength apply a second coat the following day: mould this with your fingers for an authentic finish, or simply roughen the surface after twenty-four hours with a stiff brush.

Edgings Troughs, sinks, tanks and window boxes can be enclosed with strips of natural materials such as bamboo, willow or log edging bought in a roll, cut to size and fixed with nails or strong wire twists. The same materials, or a 'picket' fence made from laths, are effective for disguising a growing bag.

MULCHES

Covering the compost in a container with a mulch (a top dressing of protective material) can have positive benefits while also improving appearances. A 2.5cm (1in) layer of grit or sharp sand round succulents and other moisture-sensitive plants improves drainage and can prevent rotting in a wet season. A mulch of dried, crushed eggshells deters slugs, while a topping of used tea leaves or coffee grounds helps maintain the acid environment enjoyed by ericaceous (lime-hating) plants such as azaleas, epimediums and trilliums (as do spent teabags to cover their drainage holes at potting time).

Flat stones or pieces of slate layered around container-grown shrubs and trees will conserve soil moisture, keep roots cool and look ruggedly appealing; or you can use organic materials like bark, cocoa shells, beech mast or small cones. Other decorative materials such as glass beads, recycled copper fragments, coloured gravels and assorted seashells can help reduce watering and deter weed invasion when used in this way.

ACCESSORIES

In addition to a stock of fresh compost and containers of various sizes and materials, pot enthusiasts will need to keep a simple selection of basic tools and ingredients.

Compost additives Included here are water gel (absorbent polymer granules), which can trap and release enormous amounts of water and is mixed into compost to delay drying out; sharp sand, grit, vermiculite and perlite, which can be added to improve drainage for plants sensitive to damp conditions; and fertilizers such as slow-release and general feeds for reviving compost after existing nutrients have been exhausted.

Larger aggregates Gravel, clay pot fragments, crushed bricks and broken polystyrene are valuable materials for drainage layers at the bottom of containers. Flat stones and pieces of slate can be used for mulching

larger containers and for wedging under pots instead of purpose-made 'feet' to level them and maintain clear drainage at the base.

Potting tools A narrow-bladed trowel is ideal for planting or you can use an old tablespoon for smaller specimens such as plug plants; a hand fork (or a table fork) is useful for loosening compost, especially in established containers where the surface has become compacted, weedy or green with algae. Add clean labels, string or raffia, garden wire, secateurs or a sharp knife, a selection of thin canes and sticks, and perhaps a pair of gloves, and your essential tool kit is complete.

2

PLACES for POTS

Context is as important as the style of pot and the type of plant it hosts. Sound practical reasons may dictate the choice of place – shelter from cold winds, perhaps, or access for regular attention – and some urban locations can be challenging. But very often it takes just a little imagination, and perhaps a sense of fun and adventure, to find the right spot and so raise a container plant from the commonplace into a thing of great beauty with a key role to play in the landscape.

Impact relies on context. Heavy wood and aluminium cubes (page 38) dominate the matching four-square structural elements of their surroundings, whereas the almost whimsically top-heavy avocado tree in its softly rounded pot (left) blends perfectly into a casual setting of pebbles, gravel and reeds.

PRACTICAL CONSIDERATIONS

Any pot or larger container that has been imaginatively conceived and skilfully made is likely to be a beautiful piece of craftsmanship on its own, even when not being used to hold a plant. Deciding a place for it then is like staging a piece of sculpture: appearance and impact are everything, and your eye will tell you when you have found the place that best flatters its good looks. A Greek pithos emerging from a sea of prostrate juniper, for instance, is a composition in its own right.

Once a container is planted up, however, priorities change and the well-being of the plants becomes paramount. Some kinds need sun, others cool shade, for example. Strong winds injure large soft foliage, damage stems and rapidly dry the contents of pots, especially those made from a porous material like clay; sudden gusts can topple tall and top-heavy plants – an important consideration on balconies and roof tops. All plants need to be within easy reach for watering and routine maintenance, which may involve making special arrangements for hanging baskets and window boxes in awkward positions.

Whatever a plant's visual appeal, always check its natural habitat and cultural requirements to make sure you can keep it happy in the chosen position. Many plants can forgive a little mismanagement, and some such as succulents and native wild flowers even tolerate neglect, but for the healthiest growth, a lighter care load and low casualty rate, choosing the ideal site right from the start is a wise precaution.

Display tips

- A single oversize container can look dramatic in a conspicuous position and offer ample rooting capacity for an equally impressive specimen plant or perhaps a whole collection of compatible plants.
- Group small pots together for maximum impact (the sum is often greater than the number of parts) and easier maintenance.
- Pots of matching or complementary shapes and materials look more of a piece than a motley collection, but vary their sizes and heights to relieve uniformity.
- A very tall container like a chimney pot can appear gaunt and forlorn on its own, and more satisfying as part of a small group of similar style.

Pots fulfil a range of dramatic roles in the garden. They can be staged as principal players – like this prominent tin tub of variegated hosta – or as extras, to vary and soften the edges of a perennial border.

POTS ON THE PATIO

A patio or paved area is like a stage and your containers the cast to be positioned in key places for dramatic effect: they can relieve the starkness of walls and slabs, and animate an otherwise lifeless built environment.

How you arrange the pots depends on the impact you want to create. Climbers, shrubs and small trees in substantial pots will clothe a wall or form a screen, while beech, bamboos or a wildlife mixture of flowering and berried native shrubs in containers marshalled in a row can merge into an effective hedge for a windbreak or to ensure seclusion and intimacy.

Decorate a blank wall with hanging pots, baskets or wire window-box inserts, securely fixed and staggered to prevent trailing foliage from smothering growth below. Many lovely climbers trail effectively, while sprawling or creeping perennials like *Persicaria affinis*, bugle (*Ajuga*) and prostrate campanulas will hang in colourful swags.

When gathered together pots successfully bridge the interface between house and garden, and make an important contribution to the view from either vantage point, so position and compose prominent groups boldly. Use larger plants like trees, shrubs and trained climbers as the main focus, and arrange smaller pots around them in a

Complete permanent gardens or seasonally changing corners can be created by gathering together a number of varied plants: rearrange them according to height or time of year, bringing any in flower forward into full view, as here.

Choreographing containers

- Select key permanent sites for trees, water gardens and similar subjects too heavy to move.
- Keep a wheeled base or low trolley to manoeuvre containers if you have to transfer them to more suitable positions or indoors for frost-protection.
- Fruit, vegetables and other sun-loving plants usually need one or more moves at certain seasons to find sun or shelter from the cold.
- Gather smaller pots into groups at inclement times of the year to make watering or protection from frost easier.
- Tender plants, drought-loving species and shallow pots that freeze easily should be moved indoors altogether in winter.
- For continuity keep a reserve of younger or successional plants to replace those past their best.

supporting role, perhaps exchanging these for others as flowering seasons pass. Stand some on upturned pots, buckets or thick logs to vary height. Remember to organize a mixed colony of useful herbs and salads for fresh pickings near the door.

Keep main walkways across the patio and access steps free from obstruction. You could flank them with an avenue of pots filled with seasonal flowers like lilies, fuchsias and tall fragrant nicotianas, cauldrons of fat hostas or rhubarb, or more permanent subjects such as box (*Buxus*) topiary balls or cordon fruit. A flight of steps is a ready-made display site for potted flowers.

Add a water feature or discreet lighting to create ambience, but do not install these irrevocably in case you need to change the layout: remember one of the main assets of container plants is mobility, and you may need the freedom to move displays to follow the sun, arrange successional flowering or simply clear space for a patio party.

DECORATING WITH CONTAINERS

Restrained plants in small pots are the bric-a-brac of garden displays, especially in patios, courtyards and similar restricted areas, and extensive collections quickly grow as more are added – there is always room for just one more small, irresistible plant.

If floor space runs out or your collection appears diminished at ground level, look around for raised sites to lift some plants closer to eye level. A wall or fence is one potential display area, where climbers in ground-level containers can blend seamlessly with hanging baskets and potted plants suspended in wire loops hooked over the laths of trellis panels.

Hang pots and baskets in groups of three or more for an impressive display. Hemispherical wire baskets, animal feed mangers, flat-backed pots and even painted tin cans can all be screwed on vertical surfaces for direct planting or as pot-holders. Plastic flower pouches and sleeves are simply hung from hooks.

Window sills and ledges are obvious platforms for pots and boxes (see page 31). The tops of low walls make convenient stands for pots and containers, or you could build troughs from timber, bricks or concrete to create a permanent wall-top garden in which to plant or plunge pots. Fixed or adjustable shelving on walls and fences can multiply display opportunities: cut out circles to hold pots securely and prevent accidents.

Free-standing units placed near a wall can reinforce the display but look equally effective in the open, especially when seen against a complementary backdrop like a distant view or a plain hedge. Traditional jardinières, a recycled saucepan stand or an old painted stepladder will offer several levels for composing a tiered display of trailers, bulbs, a collection of succulents or seasonal highlights like cascade chrysanthemums or carnations.

BASKETS AND BOXES

Wood, wire and wickerwork are materials with a natural or informal appearance that can help containers blend into their surroundings or become a passive setting for plants.

Baskets

Willow, hazel and split bamboo are just some of the materials used for traditional woven baskets, which make excellent and fairly durable containers if treated with wood preservative and fitted with a plastic lining. Particularly decorative baskets deserve staging on a table top or shelf. Some shapes are designed to hang on a wall, while larger examples such as log and laundry baskets look effective on the ground, filled with informal arrangements of herbs and cottage garden plants or a choice shrub like leycesteria or myrtle. Wire waste-paper bins serve the same purpose.

Hanging baskets are popular and versatile but need careful placing because their limited compost capacity means regular watering, sometimes twice daily in summer. All kinds are heavy when filled and watered (as much as 10kg/22lb). Suspend them from brackets anchored with plugs and screws in sound walls or from hooks on a pergola or similar overhead structure.

They look particularly festive when flanking doorways and windows, but check they are not in the way of passers-by, especially when dripping with water. Avoid windy positions and choose plants that suit the amount

Collections of bulbs such as these hippeastrum (amaryllis) hybrids and miniature narcissi thrive in pots, where they can be watered and displayed when in growth or tucked away somewhere dry while dormant.

Table-top gardening

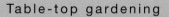

Special plants deserve simple but prominent display in table-top settings outdoors: a bowl of fragrant heliotrope or pinks, for example, a mound of flowering cacti or a trailing *Begonia sutherlandii* raised on a secure cake stand. Framing the top of an old wooden card or picnic-table with sides about 8cm (3in) deep provides a planting area for dwarf herbs, prostrate mat-forming plants or even fine lawn grasses to make a living tableau. Add slate or tile inserts as 'place mats' for food and drinks.

A sill or shelf is an inviting lodging place for a plant box. A window box can host a traditional community of bedding plants, like the petunias, ivies, lobelia and pelargoniums seen here, but could equally well serve as a home for perennial flowers all year round. *Brugmansia* (syn. *Datura*) *suaveolens* (angels' trumpets, foreground) is a typical perennial candidate for container culture, as are the evergreen sentries flanking the doorway.

49

A sun-bathed trough (left) displays glorious summer bedding to perfection. These drought-tolerant Madagascan periwinkles (*Catharanthus roseus*) are happy even in the dry rain shadow of a window reveal.

Ingenuity knows no bounds. Concrete slabs secured with packing bands (opposite) make efficient and good-looking improvised wall boxes for a late spring bedding display on a wall of matching pavers.

of sun or shade the baskets will receive. To improve access for watering you can suspend the basket from a pulley, fit an adjustable or spring-loaded chain or use a long-handled watering lance.

Hanging baskets are portable and may be brought into a greenhouse or conservatory for the winter. This allows you to extend their flowering season, or plant them with houseplants such as forest cacti and tradescantias or tender perennials like ivy-leaved pelargoniums and trailing petunias. If kept frost-free, barely moist and in good light, tender perennial bedding plants will survive winter indoors and produce useful cuttings the following spring.

Boxes

Recycled or home-made wooden boxes or crates can offer greater depth and more efficient drainage than many other large containers without their excessive weight. Their potential is infinite and depends on their capacity and shape. Seed boxes, for example, are ideal for shelf and table displays of small cacti, succulents, mosses, thrifts and miniature alpines, either boxed up directly or plunged in small pots into a filling of sharp sand. Larger boxes make capacious homes for vegetables, fruit, shrubs and trees, and can become major features to stand in strategic positions such as beside entrances and paths, especially at junctions, or at the edges of a patio or terrace. When standing large boxes next to house walls, leave a gap of 5–8cm (2–3in) to admit air and prevent damp problems.

Window boxes need thoughtful planning and placing to make sure they are safe, stable, unobtrusive and easily accessible – sills are in the 'rain shadow' of the house and rarely intercept enough rainwater, so daily watering is usually necessary in summer. They are often permanent features, so you need to consider their appearance and purpose all year round. Simple design, harmony of scale with walls and windows, and low-maintenance materials are all important factors.

A basic window box structure may also be used successfully on balconies, attached to railings, and even as roof gardens on boats.

ROOFS AND BALCONIES

Gardening up in the air depends almost entirely on the creative use of containers to supply living space for plants. A balcony can be a prime site for a miniature garden – even token railed ledges outside urban bedroom windows can accommodate a few pots to view from indoors – while a whole roof garden will offer a variety of exciting possibilities for outdoor living, a link with the natural world and a welcome oasis in the heart of the city.

Weight is a crucial factor when using containers above ground level, and it is vital to have the structural stability checked professionally before installing plants and other heavy items like furniture and paving materials. The total

Using containers allows plants to be cultivated in situations where most could not otherwise grow, whether as individual wall features (left) or completely furnishing a varied garden at rooftop level (opposite).

weight can be dispersed by standing the heaviest containers close to or immediately over load-bearing walls and on steps, while fixing others to walls, railings or parapets to relieve the floor load. Choose the lightest type of container (plastic dustbins are ideal for larger plants, for example), use pieces of polystyrene for drainage material and fill containers with soil-less compost.

Before deploying a lot of containers make sure you are not committing yourself to carrying numerous heavy cans of water up stairs. A standpipe can save effort and you could capture rainwater in butts if these do not compromise the weight loading. Exposure can be a problem, especially to wind, and you may need to provide plants with extra shelter, either by interposing more resilient

plants (see panel overleaf) or by erecting screens of polycarbonate, perforated to filter rather than obstruct wind.

Consider your surroundings, which you may not want to obscure, and place containers discreetly to frame or complement a view. Appearances from the street may be important, too: a balcony garden can improve the external appearance of the house or apartment if well managed. Remember wildlife, which is remarkably prolific in urban habitats and will be attracted even to a few small containers to feed and explore: choose fragrant and nectar-rich flowers, and install water, feeders and nesting boxes for resident birds.

Experiment with your choice of plants because the microclimate could be quite different from that at

As assertive as chimney pots against a clear blue sky, these handsome terracotta Roman vases almost eclipse their contents. Note their discreet repair with wires and straining bolts.

Wind-resistant plants

In an open position resilient species could make up your whole collection, or you could choose larger plants to provide windbreak shelter for less robust kinds. Explore species and varieties of anthemis, atriplex, box, broom, buddleja, bupleurum, dwarf pines and spruces, elaeagnus, eryngium, escallonia, heather, hebe, hellebore, holly, kniphofia, olearia, rowan, rugosa roses, statice (*Limonium*), tamarix and yew.

ground level. Drought-tolerance is a valuable quality, especially in sunny positions or on black-topped surfaces which quickly reach high temperatures. Heat rises and built-up town sites tend to be warmer than rural areas, so aerial positions in them may escape ground frosts and favour tender plant species, possibly relieving you of the need to overwinter them indoors.

SINK GARDENS

Old-fashioned stone sinks and modern glazed versions coated with hypertufa (see page 35) are ideal for growing alpine and rock garden plants that take up little space,

Sink garden plants
Seasonal flowers:

Seasonal flowers:
- spring: androsaces, cushion saxifrages, dwarf erysimums, primulas
- summer: alpine pinks, *Campanula cochlearifolia*, *Geranium dalmaticum*, prostrate thymes
- autumn: dwarf cyclamen and sedums, gentians, *Leucojum autumnale*
- winter: early crocus, snowdrops

Choice shrubs include *Genista pulchella*, *Petrophytum caespitosum*, *Rhododendron repens*, *Salix reticulata*, *Sorbus reducta*.

Containers are perfect for water gardening – impervious kinds for mini-ponds and smaller conventional pots for immersing marginal and aquatic plants (left). Large planters are excellent on waterside decking or as floating floral 'islands' (right).

require cool rooting conditions with fast drainage and benefit from surface protection against lingering dampness. They are classic garden features for key positions, usually in full sun, and look effective either singly or grouped together as a main feature, perhaps with some raised on bricks or blocks to vary surface levels and improve drainage. As they are usually very heavy, install them while they are empty. Complete the miniature landscape after planting by arranging a few small but attractive pieces of rock as outcrops on the surface, and then finish with a 2.5cm (1in) mulch of gravel or shingle.

WATER FEATURES

A garden water installation requires an impervious container to act as a reservoir. This may be any size appropriate to the style and scale of the feature, whether it is a half-barrel for water lilies, for example, or a simple shallow tray where you can float a few surface plants, tea lights or a solar-powered bubble fountain.

All fittings need siting where they are safe (water is irresistible to children), easily accessible for maintenance and enjoyment, and away from strong winds so as to

Water lilies for all depths

A host of indispensable hardy lilies is available, ranging in size from miniature cultivars for shallow bowls to vigorous kinds that need the deepest containers. Allow for a spread at least double the recommended depth.

Beautiful *Nymphaea* cultivars include:

- dwarf (minimum depth 8cm/3in): 'Froebelii', *N. x helvola*, *N. tetragona*
- small (min. 15cm/6in): 'Albatross', 'Gloriosa', 'Sioux'
- medium (min. 30cm/12in): 'Escarboucle', *N. odorata*, 'Sunrise'
- large (min. 45cm/18in): 'Attraction', 'Charles de Meurville', 'Mrs Richmond'.

Over time a variety of pots and planters can be acquired as needed to embellish a terrace or flank a set of steps: here this includes formal painted boxes and rustic half-barrels, terracotta urns, jars and long tom pots, decorated garland pots and even a classical stone urn raised on a pedestal.

prevent rapid evaporation. Avoid positions under deciduous trees if fish are to be included. Shade for part of the day moderates temperature fluctuations and can be supplied by careful choice of aspect or by including plants with floating foliage (see page 76); full sun is obviously necessary for any solar-powered device.

Site a large ornamental water container such as a glazed or stone pot or a wooden tub at ground level (but remember the considerable weight of water on a balcony or roof). Shallow containers can be displayed on tables, stands or low walls, perhaps doubling as bird baths. A plain lightweight plastic tank can be lifted closer to eye level on blocks, the supports disguised within a larger container or raised bed. Alternatively bury it to the rim in the ground, perhaps surrounded by decking or paving to make a sunken feature; arrange a series of tanks in this way along the edge of a patio to form a moat. If you plan to turn it into a bog garden for marginals and moisture-loving plants, include a few drainage holes.

For easy maintenance ensure that all features are near a water source for filling or topping – rainwater overflows may be usefully diverted to adjust container levels – and to an electricity supply if a pumped feature or lighting is included.

FOCAL POINTS

Designers often site an outstanding container or group of pots as a signpost or focal point to attract attention towards (or away from) a particular area of the garden. A pair of these might be used to flank an entrance or pathway; several matching containers can be spaced out to make an effective boundary line or a series of accents leading the eye onwards.

To work effectively a focal point must stand out significantly from its surroundings, well away from any other interesting features. It might be a tall stone urn in the centre of a lawn or at the end of a path, a Versailles box of topiary or a shapely specimen tree clear of informal surroundings, or just an arresting pot of vivid flowers close to a bland wall or dark hedge. Try staging several colourful pots at intervals within or at the front of a border to provide contrasting highlights or to relieve uniformity during a temporary lull in the display.

Choice and position of any focal point needs care and thought. The plant or pot shape or colour should contrast with the immediate surroundings or echo a similar theme near by. Its position should serve a logical purpose, whether to indicate or enhance a view, punctuate a plain background or act as a pivot on a corner or edge of an area.

Choose bold plants – vivacious summer bedding, a sculpted tree like a monkey puzzle, or an extravagant froth of miscanthus or *Cotinus coggygria*, for example – but make sure you avoid a clash of style with the pot itself. On a more

modest scale play with simple but effective visual conceits like a bowl of bright flowers such as orange eschscholzias, purple osteospermums or clear white impatiens placed as a finial to mark the end of a wall or flight of steps.

CONTAINERS UNDER GLASS

Glazed structures like porches, greenhouses and conservatories span the divide between the open garden and the specialized indoor world of houseplants. Such a halfway house has traditionally been the

Leafy perennials like hostas, acanthus and a host of different grasses can be arranged in pots of appropriate size to help populate a patio and soften the edges of its decking.

calceolarias and fuchsias can pass the winter here with minimal care: simply brush or wash their containers clean, make sure plants are pest and disease free, and then move them into a well-lit and frost-proof place. Nominally hardy plants benefit from shelter in colder regions or while they are still young – pittosporums, Mediterranean cypresses, sweet bay and agapanthus, for example. Under glass is also the best place to induce early growth on tender potted perennial bedding like coleus, impatiens, nemesias and petunias to provide new stems for you to take as cuttings in late winter and early spring.

The styles and designs of containers kept permanently outdoors are equally useful and attractive for plants kept under glass:

- glazed and terracotta pots for clivias, strelitzia, tree ferns, grevilleas and bottlebrushes (*Callistemon*)
- tubs and boxes for climbers like plumbago, streptosolen and bougainvilleas
- wooden and wire hanging baskets for orchids, columneas, epiphyllums and chlorophytums
- bowls for bulbs like lachenalias, achimenes, hippeastrums and freesias.

sanctuary for tender plants moved to safety from exposure to frost – lemon and orange trees in classic orangeries, for example, or dormant dahlias and chrysanthemums under the greenhouse staging for a winter rest. The traffic is two-way, because many tropical conservatory plants welcome a summer break in the open air, while glasshouse fruits like peaches and kumquats crop more reliably if their stems and buds are allowed to ripen in the outdoor sun.

Tender bedding plants like pelargoniums,

❸

CHOOSING PLANTS

Often garden centres and gardening guides offer a limited repertoire under the heading 'container plants'. These tend to be familiar, reliable and colourful plants, usually grown as seasonal bedding and then discarded. But an empty pot invites creativity and even daring rather than safe conformity, and the range of plants that may be grown successfully in containers, on their own or in combinations, is almost infinite. All you need is the confidence to turn an opportunity into achievement.

CONSIDERING OPTIONS

The range of plants that thrive contentedly in pots is so large that having to discriminate and make a choice may seem daunting – too many options can be as disheartening as too few.

Decide first if the container (see Chapter 1) or its position (Chapter 2) is a major influence, because this will immediately disqualify various types of plants as being unsuitable. You might not be able to provide enough space, sunlight or attentive care, or the plant's shape or behaviour might not match the container, while the proposed location may not suit its growth habit.

On the other hand you could feel so passionate about a particular plant that you're prepared to buy an appropriate container and where necessary modify the surroundings or management to keep it happy. Fortunately plants are adaptable: naturally large kinds can usually be pruned to size and root restriction controls vigour to a certain extent, and varieties with special characteristics like slow growth, small size or enhanced tolerance of environmental conditions like exposure to wind or frost are often available to help you find one that suits your purpose.

GROUPING PLANTS

A pot may be somewhere to grow a particularly bold or distinctive plant to display on its own as an outstanding specimen or solo highlight, but you can also team several compatible plants as a miniature garden, whether

Citrus trees traditionally flower and fruit well in roomy orange pots like those staged out in this formal knot garden (page 62); at the other extreme, an informal collection of varied pots and planters can be orchestrated into a complete cottage garden (right).

Buying plants

- Large specimen plants can be bought already established in containers. These tend to be expensive and harder to handle, but make an instant impression.

- Planted hanging baskets, started a month or so previously and already in bloom, are a popular buy and equally immediate in their effect.

- Many gardeners prefer to start with very small plants and either pot these on at intervals as specimens or incorporate them in larger display containers.

- Young plants in cells (plug plants) are inexpensive and the most adaptable for planting up hanging baskets, pouches and tower pots, but they need several weeks' extra growth before they will make much impact.

- It is worth watching out for overgrown and discounted samples of perennial flowers at the end of the season as it is often possible to divide these and make several smaller potfuls for low cost.

assembled in individual pots or transferred together to a
larger container as a seasonal or permanent community.
The importance of overall appearance may depend on the
plants you choose. Productivity is usually a higher priority
than good looks in a tub of vegetables, for example,
whereas visual impact can be crucial to the success of a
summer bedding display on a patio. Always stage pots
experimentally to assess the best spacing and balance
before transplanting them into a larger container.

For a more flexible arrangement keep individual plants in
their pots and simply gather them close together (note
that square pots fit more closely than round ones).
Alternatively, plunge the pots to their rims in the larger
container, either to fill gaps among permanent perennials
or to assemble a complete but adaptable display.
For an effortless but compelling show of colour, sow a
mixture of flower seeds straight into a container, scattering
them perhaps over an earlier planting of bulbs to take over

as the season finishes. Mixed annuals, colour-themed if you want a monochrome effect, annual grasses and wildflower blends are all reliable and effective. You can use containers to experiment with unusual or unfamiliar seeds. Try sowing a pinch of bedding plant or perennial seeds brought back from a holiday abroad . . .

SEASONAL POTS

For many gardeners container schemes rely mainly on bedding plants set out when young and leafy (or, in the case of bulbs, while dormant). Although these plants may be annuals, bulbs, or tender or hardy perennials, for this purpose they are displayed only for a season while in bloom, foliage plants while in leaf, before being discarded and replaced with a different batch. Hanging baskets, window boxes and wall pots are favourite homes for compact or trailing seasonal bedding.

Chosen plants may be a single variety, multiple varieties of the same genus (especially where mixed colours are required) or most often a more ambitious scheme that partners plants of different heights and habits to create a balanced but contrasting composition.

The traditional summer formula for mixed bedding uses one or more central 'dot' plants, such as cannas, variegated *Abutilon pictum* 'Thompsonii' or a standard fuchsia; a perimeter ring of trailers like helichrysum, glechoma, ivy-leaved pelargoniums or milleflora petunias; and an infill of compact flowers chosen from a wide range of easy prolific kinds, from ageratum to zinnia. In early autumn annuals are discarded – perennials too unless they are overwintered indoors – to make way for an autumn, winter or spring scheme planted up in their place.

For the simplest sequence, refill the container straight away with bulbs, primroses, forget-me-nots, wallflowers, Bellis daisies and other spring flowers. But for earlier colour you could replace or intersperse summer bedding with autumn subjects like chrysanthemums, heuchera, ceratostigma, Japanese anemones, rudbeckias and thunbergia. For winter arrangements try miniature cyclamen, trailing ivies, evergreen creeping Jenny (*Lysimachia*) and shrubs such as variegated hollies, *Viburnum davidii* and silvery *Convolvulus cneorum*, all of which will brighten the winter twilight.

Displaying collections

If you collect a particular kind of plant, consider arranging your examples together in a special display unit with several shelves, either free-standing on the ground or attached to a wall – a set of wooden steps makes an ideal improvised platform. For alpines, show auriculas, cacti and other subjects sensitive to rain, design it like an open-fronted cabinet. Plants like violas, thymes and bonsai trees can be left open to the elements. Make sure all the plants against a wall receive adequate daylight by turning them a little every few days.

Don't be afraid to mix plants of different but complementary habits, as in this arrangement where seasonal pelargoniums, fuchsias and abutilons jostle with perennial grasses, ivy, succulents and clematis in a riot of flowers and foliage.

Other seasonal themes

- Grasses: for summer and autumn colour, sow a mix of annual species or team choice perennials such as *Carex rubra*, *Milium effusum* 'Aureum', *Festuca glauca*, *Hakonechloa* and *Helictotrichon*, perhaps with a dwarf miscanthus as a centrepiece.
- New Year: combine evergreen shrubs and silver ivies in a festive arrangement with colourful shrub prunings or white-painted sticks, decked with tiny lights or outdoor candles for mid-winter frivolity.
- Tropical luxuriance: move indoor plants out for the summer, plunging them in larger containers to help retain moisture and humidity. *Monstera*, cyperus, ficus and caladiums all enjoy warm shade outside and make a lavish composition with flowering lilies or *Gloriosa superba*. Indoor cacti can be gathered together in the same way for a summer break outdoors, and make excellent drought-resistant bedding.

Shrubs and trees, such as these neatly clipped topiary cones, revel in the generous rooting volume of deep box planters: topdress annually and trim regularly to echo the clean lines of the containers.

PERENNIALS

Most summer bedding schemes use tender perennials such as pelargoniums and fuchsias (while often treating them as annuals), but hardy perennials are equally successful in pots and can even benefit from the confinement, which restrains spreading growth or potentially invasive species like houttuynia, vinca, lamium and crocosmia. Most shrubs, too, react happily to container culture provided they have enough space for steady root growth.

A single species such as hosta, alchemilla or a hydrangea can look well in pots if its foliage is sufficiently ornamental to command interest when there are no flowers. Alternatively blend them in to bulk up mixed schemes, as a green foil or for contrast of texture with other flowers.

When grown as permanent container plants, perennials will need annual pruning or tidying to clear exhausted growth or maintain a pleasing shape, together with topdressing in spring (see page 97) and possible supplementary feeding once or twice during summer. Empty out vigorous herbaceous perennials when they become pot bound (about every three or four years), divide the clumps and pot up strong young segments in fresh compost as replacements.

Easy and attractive perennials include acanthus, aquilegia, dicentra, doronicum, hemerocallis, pulmonaria and stachys. Suitable shrubs include bamboos, buddleja, camellia, choisya, cordyline, elaeagnus, euonymus, hebe, hypericum, lavandula, pieris, ribes, santolina, skimmia, weigela and yucca.

TREES FOR IMPACT

Growing a tree in a pot might seem an impossible challenge, but few species are as demanding as you might suspect, provided you can supply a stable, well-drained container large enough to support healthy and unchecked growth. Once a tree grows too large to repot, simply topdress it every spring with fresh compost (see page 97) and prune the canopy to limit its size and shadow, and to maintain a pleasing shape – as the biggest plant in your display, a tree will always attract instant critical appraisal, so appearance can be crucial.

Even normally fast-growing tree species like birch and willow can be induced to mature slowly and give pleasure for years simply by rationing their food and space. Look in any woodland and you will find tree seedlings many years old, marking time until an opening overhead triggers further growth. An extreme version of this is bonsai (literally 'planted in a small pot'), an art that stunts the growth even of normally giant forest trees by restricting

Plants with bold or intriguing foliage, such as ferns and hostas (right) or spiky pandanus (far right), can look at ease in the most contemporary containers, whether brightly painted cubes, florists' water buckets or voluminous cisterns.

their root development. Traditional contorted bonsai styles are deliberately induced, whereas a tree in a tub or large container will have a normal, though miniaturized, appearance.

Choose a tree for its character and individuality. It might be a conifer to contribute its distinctive evergreen shape to the winter landscape or undergo artistic pruning, or a deciduous species to signal the different seasons with flushes of blossom, fruit and foliage that may assume vivid autumn tints before it falls. Explore different cultivars: prostrate kinds for lateral growth, weeping forms for airy gracefulness, slim fastigiate varieties for emphasis in a small space.

Easy trees for pots

Abies koreana, Japanese maples (*Acer palmatum*), birches (*Betula*), *Caragana arborescens* 'Pendula', *Cornus controversa* 'Variegata', *Gleditsia triacanthos*, Japanese cedars (*Cryptomeria*), *Larix kaempferi*, crab apples (*Malus*), *Pinus densiflora*, *Prunus incisa*, *Rhus typhina*, rowans (*Sorbus*), *Taxus baccata* 'Fastigiata'.

POTTED CLIMBERS

Like trees, climbers add valuable height and substance to a container garden. Vigorous kinds need substantial pots to provide adequate rooting space, stability for a possibly large canopy of topgrowth and long intervals between repotting or topdressing (keeping disturbance to a minimum is recommended where plants are trained and supported). A wisteria, for example, needs a tub at least 60cm (2ft) deep and wide to adorn a house wall with two or three tiers of healthy flowering branches.

A climber can be grown on its own as a star soloist or act as an anchor plant in a large container with a collection of plants. Climbers have practical structural value as screens or for camouflaging expanses of fence or wall. Away from existing structures, they need sturdy free-standing supports such as stakes, spiral metal rods, tripods or cylinders of willow, brushwood or netting. Species that twine or cling with tendrils – clematis, morning glories, runner beans, sweet peas, for example – can be left to find their own way up supports. Other kinds have evolved to scramble through obliging neighbours, and such climbers as roses, Japanese wineberries or jasmine need tying in securely at intervals if grown away from supporting plants.

When growing a climber against an upright structure such as a pergola pillar or a house wall, first attach trellis, mesh or a series of taut wires to help twiners and scramblers gain height. More independent climbers like Virginia creeper, ivy and *Hydrangea petiolaris* attach

Handle colour with courage. Gardeners cheerfully deploy the brightest flowers round the garden but cling cautiously to sombre plain containers when they could choose pots that are colourful features in their own right. Here, bright orange pots are daringly partnered with rich red tulips and daisies.

Versatile ivy

Do not underestimate ivy (*Hedera* species), which is easy to maintain and justly popular. There are hundreds of cultivars with appealing leaf markings and shapes, from large robust 'Buttercup' and 'Glacier' to charming, short-jointed miniatures that slowly develop into dense swags of dainty foliage – 'Melanie' or 'Prof. Friedrich Tobler', for example. Use fast-growing kinds for covering and screening, smaller-leaved types as trailers, ground cover under taller plants or for tying on wire formers to make leafy topiary. Vigorous ivies produce impressive formal standards after four to six years' training if you tie the main stem to an upright cane and top it regularly about 60–90cm (2–3ft) high to encourage a bushy canopy.

---

themselves directly to the surface with aerial roots or suckers and need little assistance, but remember they could be difficult or even impossible to remove and re-attach easily when decorating the surface or repotting. When planting against a wall, position the climber at the back of its container and then fill in with shorter perennials or bedding around the front.

Many shrubs will behave as though they were climbers when grown next to a vertical surface: vigorous kinds like *Cotoneaster horizontalis* or *Euonymus fortunei* 'Emerald 'n' Gold' could even reach the top of ground-floor doorways and windows if trained on wires.

BULBS AND BULBOUS PLANTS

A bulb is a complete package of dormant leaves and flower buds, waiting in a safe and convenient form for the ideal conditions to trigger growth. There are several different kinds: true bulbs like daffodils, lilies and tulips, corms (crocus, freesias, gladioli), tubers (anemones and cyclamen), rhizomes (agapanthus, cannas) and tuber-like roots (alstroemerias and dahlias).

All offer predictable performance the first season after planting in pots, and with adequate feeding after flowering will continue to please and even multiply in the years that follow. For a single season there's no need to plant them as deeply as recommended in the garden.

Because most have a concentrated flush of bloom with quite plain foliage at other times, they are ideal container plants for special display centre-stage while at their best, moving them to the side-lines as they fade.

Spring-flowering bulbs are particular favourites, heralding the welcome start of a new season in most gardens. Popular early kinds for pots include crocuses, cyclamen (especially *C. coum*), winter aconites and snowdrops. To extend the display plant these in large containers above a deeper layer of later bulbs like narcissi, scillas, hyacinths, leucojums and tulips (see panel page 75).

More bulb themes

- Explore the various kinds of summer bulbs, which may be grown on their own or under summer bedding to hide their fading foliage. Some are hardy perennials – erythroniums and galtonias, which blend easily with other plants, for example, or agapanthus, nerines and schizostylis, which prefer containers to themselves. Others are tender and need lifting every autumn for frost-free storage: these include gaudy ixias, gladioli, sparaxis and tigridias.

- Lilies combine stately growth, heady fragrance and extravagant form with reliability and an undemanding care regime. Some, like *Lilium auratum,* form stem roots and benefit from extra deep pots. All resent waterlogging and should be allowed to dry out almost completely between waterings. Buy a few top-size bulbs each year, flower them once in pots and then plant them out in undisturbed potfuls to establish in the garden.

Just half a dozen bulbs of a particular variety can produce a bowlful of beauty. When growing in confined volumes of compost, all bulbs need frequent watering and regular feeding after flowering until their leaves die down.

- Dwarf and alpine bulbs like miniature narcissi, rarer crocuses and choice cyclamen grow best in shallow pans filled with a substantial drainage layer, topped with soil-based compost and a final mulch of sharp sand or grit. Plunge pans in a cold frame or raised bed that can be covered overhead to protect bulbs while dormant, or simply store them dry in a cool shed where they are safe from damp and vermin.

PLANTS IN PANS

While large containers are mainly used to accommodate deep-rooting plants like trees, shrubs, maincrop vegetables and more vigorous perennial flowers, many smaller plants are best displayed in shallower containers. The reduced volume of compost these hold suits alpine, rockery and scree species, dwarf bulbs and other shallow-rooting subjects that might easily rot off in more lavish conditions.

Planting depth varies according to the size of the dormant bulb, and containers should be selected to reflect these differences. Narcissus bulbs, for example, need considerably more space than diminutive *Iris reticulata*.

Half-pots, pans and bowls with a much greater surface area than depth are all suitable, as are alpine sinks. All need raising off the ground to ensure good drainage and exclude pests such as slugs, and also to bring miniature details closer to eye level. Adapt the compost to the type of plant, especially for alpines and rock plants, which prefer plenty of drainage material and a soil-based compost reinforced with 25 per cent grit.

Planting ideas

- collections of a single genus such as sempervivum, echeveria, androsace, sedum or saxifraga in a gravel-topped sink
- mat-forming plants like alpine pinks, thrift and thymes to create a green landscape of tufts, mounds and hummocks

Multiple planting

For an impressively full display, plant bulbs in two or three tiers, one above another and separated by a layer of compost just deep enough to cover the tips of lower bulbs. Single varieties can be massed in this way, or you could plant a strong species such as tulips in the deepest layer and finish with a smaller bulb like crocus, which prefers to be nearer the surface.

- pans of soil-less lime-free compost mixed with equal amounts of coffee grounds and tea leaves (which are naturally acid) to grow mosses and carnivorous bog plants
- bowls of miniature bulbs like species crocus, cyclamen, sisyrinchiums and dwarf irises and narcissi to bring indoors while flowering
- pans of dwarf conifers like *Juniperus communis* 'Compressa' and tiny shrubs such as *Genista pulchella* or *Salix reticulata* for a mountain landscape in miniature.

WATER PLANTS

Most pond and bog plants adapt successfully to pot culture provided the compost and drainage is tailored to their often specialized lifestyle. Their common requirement is for moisture at the roots, but the degree of wetness depends on the type of plant and its preferred habitat.

Deep water aquatics Water lilies, golden club (*Orontium*), pickerel weed (*Pontederia*) and similar true aquatics live away from the banks and need depths of 15cm (6in) or more where they can root freely in a bottom layer of soil or grow in open baskets of special compost (see panel).

Floaters These are free-drifting species, including tender plants like water lettuce (*Pistia stratiotes*) with its neat rosettes of velvety leaves, and hardier plants such

The smallest waterproof container can be used to make an appealing water feature to please gardeners and wildlife alike, and will provide a surprise for visitors if it is tucked secretively out of immediate view.

as frogbit (*Hydrocharis*) and the peculiar carnivorous bladderwort (*Utricularia*). Use them to decorate the surface of table-top bowls, pans and deeper containers of still water.

Marginals These live in shallow water or root into wet banks, and may be potted up in the usual way provided you keep the compost wet by standing containers in saucers topped up with water. Easy species in this large group include marsh marigolds (*Caltha palustris*), arrowhead (*Sagittaria*) and the striped foliage plant sweet flag (*Acorus calamus* 'Variegatus'). Gunnera looks handsome and astonishing in large bold containers.

Bog plants A terrestrial group that needs constantly moist but not always waterlogged compost. Large containers stay moist for longer. Make sure they have holes at the base, but omit the usual drainage layer when potting and fill them with soil-less compost fortified with water-retentive gel. The huge range includes many familiar garden plants like astilbes, hemerocallis, houttuynia and rodgersia.

CONTAINER CROPS

Plants in pots need not be restricted to flowers, and many gardeners successfully raise a great range of kitchen garden crops in all kinds of containers, from baskets and window boxes to deep plastic potato bags and drums or wooden crates for fruit trees and maincrop roots. Many container crops need a little more attention than ornamentals, because quality and often timing can be important.

A pond in a pot

To make true aquatic plants happy, keep them in a mini-pond in an impermeable container such as a large glazed pot, at least 45cm (18in) diameter, or a half-barrel lined with plastic or a piece of flexible pond liner if the staves are not reliably watertight. Pot up plants in perforated water-plant baskets filled with aquatic plant compost, and immerse them on bricks or upturned pots at their preferred depths. For a moving water feature, float a solar-powered bubble fountain on the surface and grow splash-tolerant marginals near by, such as creeping Jenny (*Lysimachia*), mimulus and water dropwort (*Oenanthe*). Add an oxygenator like willow moss (*Fontinalis*) or hairgrass (*Eleocharis*) for water clarity.

Vegetables

Most vegetables are easy to grow in pots, tubs, window boxes and even hanging baskets, provided they have a large enough volume of compost to prevent untimely drying out and to support unchecked root development. It is important therefore to match crop to container. Comparatively restrained landcress and miniature tomatoes will thrive in a hanging basket, for example, whereas courgettes are greedy and vigorous, and for healthy growth and steady cropping need about 40 litres (9 gallons) of compost per plant in a container at least 30cm (12in) deep.

For maximum economy choose the largest container you have for kitchen garden crops. Plant this with one or two bulky heavy feeders, or turn it into a miniature kitchen garden, with climbing beans or sweetcorn in the centre, perhaps, surrounded by shorter plants like leaf beet (perpetual spinach) and salad rocket teamed with trailing lobelia, tagetes to deter some insect pests and edible flowers such as pot marigolds, pansies or variegated nasturtiums.

Take advantage of containers' mobility to station them where they receive the right amount of sun and heat. Summer-fruiting crops like tomatoes, peppers and aubergines revel on sunny patios, while leafy vegetables such as spinach, lettuce and claytonia prefer cool shade in high summer. If possible, find space in the garden for a cold frame or seedbed where you can start follow-on sowings in cell trays or small pots to replace those in the main containers once they have been harvested.

Choose varieties with care, concentrating on dwarf and compact kinds that not only occupy less space but also require less water: total yields might be less but their management is not as demanding. As a further precaution select immune, tolerant and resistant varieties (sometimes listed as 'ideal for organic gardeners') to reduce the need to tackle pests or diseases. Gather crops while still young and tender, replace them promptly with successional batches, and move them into the sun early and late in the year to prolong the harvest.

Herbs

The majority of common culinary herbs make excellent container subjects, which can be an advantage if you can position them near a door or window for convenient picking. Plant up two or three pots of each of your favourites and use them in rotation, cropping one while others recover and develop new growth to harvest later.

Their requirements are simple: few are greedy or demanding plants, most prefer full sun, moderate fertility and good drainage, and only some of the more vigorous kinds need large containers. Most are happy in a 15–20cm (6–8in) pot, or you can gather several plants together in a single container – a mixture of useful kinds in a sink or trough to make a miniature herb garden, perhaps, or different varieties of a particular herb like thyme or marjoram in a tall strawberry pot or a window box. A herb like mint or tarragon benefits from pot culture, which restrains the creeping roots that would otherwise

Tomatoes enjoy generous root space, as in this deep box, but taste best when their feeding is limited, so mop up surplus nitrogen by adding leafy salads or parsley as companions.

Special crops

Some vegetables are particularly suited to container cultivation.

- Growing carrots in large drums at least 60cm (24in) high can protect them from carrot flies, which cruise below that height when searching for sites to lay their eggs.

- Save tubers from an early potato harvest (or buy specially prepared 'second crop' tubers) and plant them in late summer in large buckets or tubs half-filled with a mixture of garden soil and compost. Add more to earth up stems as they grow. Harvest crops in late autumn, or keep containers dry under cover until Christmas as an improvised store.

- Deep Versailles boxes are ideal for growing asparagus, which appreciates the light friable texture and good drainage of potting compost; if you garden on clay this may be the only way to grow it. Stop cutting spears at the longest day, and instead enjoy (or cut for vases) the lavish display of fronds that unfurl for the rest of the season.

invade an ever-increasing area of open ground.

For best results choose varieties that combine good flavour with an attractive appearance – many herbs occur in variegated forms, with handsome gold, silver, red or cream markings on a green background. Match their beauty with a choice container of appropriate shape and material. Add 1 part sharp sand to 4 parts compost to make a well-drained mix for all but a few leafy kinds such as parsley, angelica and lovage, which prefer cool, moist conditions in light shade. Stand the others in full sun.

Harvest regularly, pinching off the young growing tips to encourage further branching: you can dry these for storing if they are not needed immediately. Sow fresh supplies of annual and biennial herbs (basil, chervil, dill, parsley, for example) every spring, and renew perennials like sage and thyme by taking cuttings every three or four years. Woody herbs like rosemary, lavender and bay can be potted on until established in large containers – about 45cm (18in) minimum diameter – after which they only need topdressing or repotting every few years.

Fruit

Growing fruit in pots is an ancient art that allowed professional gardeners to show off their skill and precision in training and pruning. Potted grape vines bearing ripe bunches were presented at table, and ornamentally trained apples or pears in flower or fruit would line paths and walks.

One of the most successful and ornamental fruits for pot culture, a fig can be even more productive than usual when its vigorous roots are confined from wandering far and wide.

Modern methods have brought fruit culture in containers within the reach of every gardener, although some varieties are still difficult: pears tend to be too large and vigorous to tolerate root restriction, grapes need careful attention to avoid plenty of foliage and no fruit, and raspberries are difficult to manage. But other kinds are a practical proposition if you choose the best forms.

Most need a container at least 38cm (15in) deep, and prefer soil-based compost to soil-less mixes. Top (or tree) fruit should be grafted on a rootstock that firmly restricts size and growth rate: apples are best on M27 or M9 stocks, cherries on 'Colt' or 'Inmil', peaches and plums on 'Pixy'. With the exception of genetically dwarf peaches, nectarines and apricots, which naturally produce small bushes, all need training to further limit growth – peaches, plums and cherries as bushes or fans trained against a wall, apples as cordons, dwarf pyramids or family trees with several varieties on a single plant. You should also check if a variety fruits on its own (is self-fertile) or needs another compatible variety near by for cross-pollination.

Soft fruit is often more straightforward. Gooseberries and red- or whitecurrants grow easily as bushes or short standards (with a single main stem like a small tree) and crop freely with simple annual pruning; blueberries are very happy in pots of acid (ericaceous) compost; figs actually fruit more heavily when their roots are confined; and rhubarb makes a large lush clump of shapely foliage if topdressed annually with manure.

Favourite and easiest of all fruit for containers is the strawberry, which succeeds in very little space and can be cropped in growing bags, window boxes, hanging baskets or pots only 15cm (6in) across. A strawberry barrel or tower allows several plants to be grown together in a small space, with the fruit held clear of the ground. Summer-fruiting varieties bear for only a few weeks, whereas perpetual (ever-bearing) and alpine kinds fruit in flushes from summer until the frosts.

All fruits need watering consistently (but guard against excess) when in flower and while ripening their crops, regular feeding and annual topdressing, and protection from birds and squirrels while the fruit ripens. Strawberries are replaced after three years with fresh bought plants or young plantlets taken from runners produced in summer. Other fruits will usually crop for many years.

MANAGING CONTAINERS

Most plants have evolved to fend for themselves in open ground, where their roots can venture where they choose in search of natural sources of food and water. When grown in a pot, however, a plant is confined in a very limited space with finite resources, and depends on you for its sustenance. But being responsible for the well-being of container plants is neither demanding nor difficult, and most gardeners find catering for them compulsive and rewarding.

MEDIA MATTERS

Plants in containers cannot thrive for long in ordinary soil, unless you are very lucky with your type of garden. Most kinds provide insufficient aeration or drainage and an unbalanced supply of nutrients, and their deficiencies become very obvious in the restricted artificial conditions of a pot. Instead you have to use specially formulated seed or potting composts (often generically called growing media), which are designed to supply all the key ingredients for steady, healthy plant growth. Alternatively you can mix your own, as gardeners have done for generations (see below).

A good container compost combines several vital properties:

- a stable structure that retains moisture while encouraging any excess to drain away safely
- a friable texture, admitting sufficient air for the roots to function properly
- a balanced supply of nutrients in a form readily available to the plant
- freedom from soil pests and diseases
- consistent, uniform and predictable performance.

Making your own potting mixture

If your garden soil is crumbly, pleasant to handle and drains well, and also allows plants to grow well, it can form the basis of a home-made potting medium. Only use the topsoil, the upper 15–20cm (6–8in), and sieve

this well to remove stones and weed roots. Mix equal proportions of sieved soil, leafmould and mature garden compost thoroughly with your hands for small amounts or a spade for larger quantities.

If you have no leafmould or garden compost, an alternative recipe is 3 parts sieved soil, 2 parts peat (but see panel on page 86) and 1 part sharp sand. Mix these together, and to every 10 litres (2 gallons) add 60g (2oz) general fertilizer (see page 98), plus 15g (½oz) garden lime unless the soil is already chalky, and mix thoroughly.

Soil-based mixtures stay moist for longer and need less frequent watering, contain some natural nutrients, have a consistent and permanent structure similar to the best garden soil, and weigh heavier, an advantage wherever containers need to be stable. Standard JI mixtures are available in different grades, as seed, cuttings and potting composts depending on the ratio of their ingredients.

Soil-less composts dry more easily and can be difficult to re-moisten if left dry for long. They need regular supplementary feeding, feel pleasant to handle but eventually break down (especially if compacted or allowed to dry out) and weigh less, except when very moist, so they are a good choice for window boxes, hanging baskets and containers on balconies. They are usually sold in a 'universal' or 'multi-purpose' formulation for general use.

Various special composts can be bought, including:

- ericaceous, an acid mixture for lime-hating plants such as rhododendrons, pieris, heathers and blueberries
- cactus, a porous and gritty blend for cacti, succulents, alpines and other plants that need very free-draining conditions
- bulb, a fibrous blend, usually with added charcoal to maintain a good growing environment even in containers without drainage holes.

Creating a seasonal flower show makes the most of containers – a spring display of tulips, pansies and wallflowers (page 82) can quickly be replaced with summer bedding such as pelargoniums (above), here waiting in the wings on greenhouse staging.

Buying compost

Commercially produced compost is either soil-based (usually labelled 'John Innes' or 'JI' if made to a standard recipe) or soil-less, with the soil fraction replaced by peat or a similar fibrous, moisture-retentive material. Each kind has particular virtues.

The problem with peat

Peat is the decayed remains of mosses and other bog plants, and a finite resource. Its continued extraction is steadily destroying rare and fragile wildlife habitats. Peat-free composts contain substitute materials, usually waste products of various kinds that often behave subtly differently from peat, so treat these with caution until you are familiar with their performance. 'Reclaimed' peat is a natural deposit filtered from streams to prevent water-flow problems, and its production does not harm the environment. One of the best substitutes is leafmould, easily made at home from autumn tree leaves gathered up and kept to rot down for a year or two in a wire mesh enclosure outdoors. Small amounts can be packed in perforated black plastic bin liners, where the leaves decay quickly, especially if mixed with some fresh lawn mowings to activate decomposition.

The business of potting plants and their routine care is pleasant, relaxing work for a sunny afternoon. When waterproofed, a halved wooden tub makes a fitting rustic pond feature.

Using old compost

Out-of-date compost and any salvaged from repotting is too valuable to discard, and may be used in a number of ways.

- Fork it into seed and nursery beds outdoors to improve the drainage and friability of your garden soil for young plants.
- Include it in compost heaps to add mineral and fibrous ingredients to the final mix.
- Use it in the lower half of larger containers, below the immediate rooting zone where fresh compost is essential.
- Save it for covering in seed drills after sowing, especially on heavy, slow-draining and impoverished soils.

When using any kind of compost, make sure it is uniformly moist, a comfortable temperature to avoid chilling plants, and fresh – using up a previous year's supply for potting can be false economy because the feed ingredients deteriorate as they age (see panel). Close bags securely after use to prevent drying out and to exclude pests, earthworms and weed seeds.

DRAINAGE

Waterlogged compost can inhibit or injure the roots of most plants by excluding air and encouraging stagnation, resulting in a number of disorders. Avoid these by making sure all outdoor containers have plenty of drainage holes at their base. Cover these at potting time with a generous layer of coarse drainage material to prevent

All the essential materials for successful container gardening are assembled here: pots of various depths and capacities, fresh compost to hand on the potting bench, seeds of every kind, and the vital notebook to record their progress.

them from becoming blocked by compacted compost.

Suitable materials include coarse gravel, small stones, broken clay pots (crocks), or roughly crumbled polystyrene (a lightweight alternative for wind-free sites). Fill about one-tenth of the depth of the pot, increasing this amount up to a third or even halfway for large deep containers requiring extra stability in exposed positions.

Plants such as succulents, many herbs, Mediterranean subjects and alpines are particularly sensitive to excess water, so reinforce the effect of a generous basal drainage layer by adding about 25 per cent fine grit, sharp sand or vermiculite to the compost to increase its porosity.

Aquatic and moisture-loving plants, on the other hand, prefer wetter conditions and can often tolerate pure garden soil (unless this is very fine and sandy). Simply sieve out stones, sticks and weed roots, add some grit to improve texture if the soil is mainly stiff clay, and then mix in bonemeal at about 60g (2oz) per 10 litres (2 gallons) to make an acceptable blend.

True aquatic and marginal plants like flag irises and white arum lilies (*Zantedeschia*) enjoy the constant moisture supplied by standing containers in saucers kept part-filled with a little water (a useful emergency measure

Being firm with compost

Soil-based mixtures have always been firmed lightly to exclude air pockets and to avoid later settlement in the pot. Plants such as chrysanthemums can even stand being rammed all round their stems with a trowel handle to encourage sturdy growth, but they are special cases. Trees and shrubs appreciate firmer planting than most herbaceous species.Only push soil-less composts down lightly, however, because firmer planting can cause compaction and airlessness. Simply settle the filled pot by knocking it sharply several times on a hard surface, and then thoroughly water in the plant with a watering can fitted with a rose.

for any plant if you are away for several days). Saucers can also prevent annoying drips from overhead containers and surplus water from running over vulnerable surfaces.

For more terrestrial species, however, saucers may be potentially harmful unless checked regularly and any standing water emptied. Most plants benefit from totally unimpeded drainage, best guaranteed by raising containers on pieces of slate or crock or on ornamental feet so that their drainage holes are clear of the ground.

Although often used to isolate and coddle difficult or exotic species, pot culture also suits many robust everyday (but equally lovely) flowers such as these aptly named double pot marigolds (*Calendula officinalis* 'Orange King').

With careful pruning, watering and topdressing, fruit trees like the various types of citrus will be content for many years in spacious containers, eventually growing into shapely mature specimens.

POTTING

Although most garden species are more resilient than you might suspect, a little extra care at potting time will reap benefits later from contented plants. Potting and planting methods vary slightly depending on the particular plant or container, but some simple rules apply to all.

- Make sure the container is clean and the compost suitable for the plant.
- Water the plant well and leave to drain thoroughly before starting.
- Choose a time when plants are in active growth and better able to recover quickly from the move.
- Handle plants confidently but sensitively, and avoid disturbing their roots unnecessarily.
- Always finish with the plant at the same depth as it was growing before you started.

Planting large containers

- To make work less strenuous, move the empty container into its final position and wedge off the ground with pieces of slate or shaped 'feet'. Make sure the drainage holes are clear and cover them with a deep layer of gravel, crocks or similar coarse material.

Grasses are a diverse group of ornamental, often graceful plants, many of them fattening into spreading clumps of arching foliage that need a prominent position to do them full justice.

- Fill the container with fresh moist compost – for large containers use a universal soil-less mix or John Innes No. 3. Fill to the top and then lightly firm with your fingers to leave the surface about 5cm (2in) below the top (adding plants will raise the final level).

- Most plants will be growing in pots and have established rootballs with plenty of roots all round the sides. Stage plants in their old pots on the surface of the compost in the new container to approve spacing and combination. Gently tap the pot to loosen the plant and carefully lift it out ready for planting. Scoop out a hole where the plant is to grow, large enough for a snug fit, and firm the plant in place.

- For multiple plantings, start with the central plant (usually the largest or tallest) and then add smaller plants all round, finishing with any edging or trailing plants at the sides. You can use the pots to gauge hole size and position before planting. Water in everything gently and tuck any vital labels discreetly at the side of the container.

See also How to plant a basket (page 30), and Strawberry tower (pages 32–3).

Potting a bare-root plant

The main precaution to take here is avoiding damaging unprotected roots.

- Prime the pot with an adequate drainage layer and then fill almost to the rim with the appropriate compost (see pages 84–6).
- When potting a seedling or young plant, scoop out a central hole with your fingers, large enough to accommodate the roots comfortably.
- Hold the plant in position with one hand and with the other sprinkle compost round and between the roots, up to the original growing depth.
- Tap the pot to settle the contents, level the surface to leave a 1cm (½in) watering space below the rim and water in gently.

With a larger plant, such as a bare-root tree, use the same method but only part-fill the pot before standing the plant inside to test its depth. Add more compost and then gently shake the plant to settle compost between its roots. Firm the compost and continue filling the pot in stages to the top, leaving a level surface with space for watering.

Potting on

When a plant's roots have filled all the available space (that is, it has become pot bound) and are starting to emerge through the drainage holes, it is time to pot it on into a larger container. Other cues are slower growth, rapid drying out and roots visible at the surface.

Potting on can be done any time during the growing season. The next size of pot should be about 5cm (2in) wider and deeper than the previous one, even if this gradual enlargement means potting on again later in the season: transfer to a much larger pot can be counter-productive, resulting in the plant sulking unhappily in an excessive volume of compost that stays wet and discourages root growth.

The following method is virtually foolproof:

- Crock the new pot with drainage material and cover this with a layer of fresh compost.
- Stand the potted plant in the centre and adjust its level by adding or removing compost until the plant is at the right depth.
- Pack compost all round the plant and gently firm it with your fingers or tap to settle it.
- Twist the potted plant round gently until it can be lifted out without disturbing the compost 'mould'.
- Knock the plant from its pot and transfer to the moulded hollow.
- Firm lightly all round, tap the new pot on a hard surface to settle the contents, level and water.

Repotting and topdressing

If a plant is pot bound and you do not want to move it on to a larger container, it will need repotting in a pot of the same size. As this involves disturbing and pruning the rootball, it is best done while the plant is dormant, usually in mid- to late winter.

Knock the plant out and carefully shake off any loose compost. Scrape more from the rootball with a hand or table fork and also trim off any dead roots and some of the live root tips until the rootball is reduced in size by about one-quarter. Then pot it up with fresh compost in a clean pot of the original size.

Where the plant or container is too big or heavy to manipulate easily, topdressing offers an alternative method of refreshing the compost. Using a hand fork and trowel, loosen and remove the top 5cm (2in) of old compost, and replace this with a fresh supply.

WATERING

Plants in garden containers are generally less demanding than houseplants, which are subjected to extra stresses such as central heating, draughts and lack of light, and often need even less attention than those growing in the open ground, with the notable exception of watering.

Providing just the right amount of water at the right time is a skill learned only from experience. Too much can be potentially as harmful as too little, but sound potting techniques help ensure against misjudgement.

A generous drainage layer and a well-balanced compost in a pot standing clear of the ground helps compensate for occasional over-watering.

Giving too little can be a greater danger in a dry summer or where smaller containers are exposed to hot sunshine or drying winds. Adding water-retentive gel (see page 37) to the compost delays drying out, although watering once, even twice a day in high summer may still be necessary. It is always advisable to check regularly and consistently.

Inspect all containers in the morning, before the sun reaches them, or in the evening as temperature and sunlight decline – during the heat of the day water can scorch foliage and often evaporates before it can reach all the roots. Water generously with a can until the excess runs from the drainage holes. If a pot is very dry or bubbles at the surface when watered from above, stand it in a tray of water for an hour or two to rehydrate from below.

Self-watering containers can reduce the need for frequent checks, as will an automatic watering system using adjustable individual drip lines connected to a tap, ideally with a programmable timer. Remember, though, that this will operate even in rain, so be alert to changes in the weather.

FEEDING

The fertilizers included in bought composts are often quickly exhausted, especially when frequent watering or rainfall leaches the soluble nutrients from containers as they drain. Special slow-release feeds are available for mixing in at potting time and these can last all season, but plants in standard composts usually need supplementary feeding from about six weeks after potting or planting.

For routine use every ten to fourteen days during the growing season, ignore specific fertilizers and choose instead a general or balanced feed containing a full complement of minor (trace) elements as well as all the major nutrients. A sound standby is tomato fertilizer, a high-potash feed valuable where flower and fruit development is preferable to lush foliar growth.

Feeding guide

- For fast results, water with soluble or liquid feeds, and use powders or granules for a slower, long-lasting effect.
- Fertilizer sticks, pellets and tablets are slow-release feeds that are simply pushed into the compost, one or more per pot.
- Nutrients can be absorbed only when dissolved, so be sure to water before or after application as directed.
- Reduce feeding as growth slows down in autumn, refrain altogether in winter, and resume as spring growth revives.

A range of plant supports, from simple canes to elaborate and decorative basketwork tepees, is available for keeping plants organized and tidy; but always choose containers that are deep enough to guarantee their stability.

SUPPORTING PLANTS

Tall, weak-stemmed and climbing plants in containers need timely and unobtrusive support to avoid spoiling their display. Always provide this before the plant is in real need because it is rarely possible to salvage wayward growth tidily.

Stout canes or a central stake can look ungainly or become unstable. A neater solution is to insert several slender canes or brushwood around the rim of the pot, joining these with loops of raffia or soft string. Alternatively push in three or four evenly spaced canes and gather them at the top to make a pyramid for climbers and bushy herbaceous plants.

Various proprietary hoops, wire rings and mesh panels are often more effective in shallow or broad containers, and special frames are available to support plants in growing bags. Climbers are best trained on tripod or pyramid-shaped frames, or can be grown on wires or trellis attached to a wall.

GROOMING

Most garden plants need occasional trimming and tidying, but those in containers benefit most from grooming because of their high visibility; plants in isolation need to look good from all sides.

Pinching out growing tips and shortening or removing excessively long shoots will ensure bushy growth and a symmetrical appearance. Deadheading spent flowers tidies plants and helps keep them disease-free as well as often encouraging more blooms by preventing energy being wasted in seed production. Many plants also require pruning once or twice a year to maintain a healthy balance between topgrowth and the inevitably restricted root development, and also to stimulate the growth of fresh replacement shoots.

FIRST AID

Plants in containers are subject to the same pests and diseases as any open-ground relative, but their privileged position means they are more readily inspected and treated when first signs appear.

Very often ailments are the result of cultural errors like overwatering, exposure to frost or starvation, and these rarely turn out to be serious. A few basic precautions, recognizing early signs and taking prompt action will usually prevent major problems from developing.

Seasonal precautions

Many people take holidays in summer, just when container care becomes a daily necessity. If you are going away, assemble pots in sheltered shade, where they will not dry out so quickly, and arrange for someone to take over watering responsibilities; alternatively stand full buckets of water close by and duct water to pots with dampened wicks of rope or absorbent material. Water and feed before you go away, deadhead all exhausted flowers and pick any ripe or nearly ripe produce.

Winter can bring the serious risk of frost, which may be lethal if rootballs are allowed to freeze solid. Bring tender plants under cover, gather others together for easy protection en masse and enclose single containers or complete groups with several thicknesses of bubble plastic, sacking or mats; shroud vulnerable branches with horticultural fleece and clad main stems with foam pipe insulation.

ESSENTIAL HEALTH CARE

- Choose a container of the right width and depth for the rootball – too small and roots may dry out rapidly, while too large can result in their rotting.
- Buy only healthy plants and look out for varieties recommended for container culture; inspect regularly for signs of stress or ill-health.
- Pot carefully in the appropriate compost and at the right time. As a rough guide, pot up or pot on plants in active growth and repot while they are dormant.
- Check and water regularly, perhaps twice daily in really hot weather, but only ever water if plants need it. Feed regularly in the growing season, but reduce the frequency after the longest day.
- Quarantine sick plants for treatment in a sheltered place, away from extreme heat or cold, to prevent spread of any infection. Pick off yellowing leaves and dead flowers, look for pests and rub or wash them off, and remove obviously diseased foliage.
- Accept that no plant is immortal: as an insurance take cuttings from any healthy growth and root in water or porous compost in case your intensive care fails.

The most serious pests

Woodlice will thrive in dry containers, and slugs may lurk under pots by day but are easily deterred with a mulch of grit or dried, crushed eggshells. Possibly the worst villain is the vine weevil, an increasing menace whose grub-like larvae revel in container compost (especially soil-less kinds) where they are safe from predators. They feed voraciously on almost any plant's roots, targeting cyclamen, strawberries, primulas, geums and bergenias in particular, and eventually kill unless detected. The large, slow-moving black adult weevils feed on leaves, causing telltale semicircular marginal holes – they can often be found and destroyed on foliage after dark, especially in late spring as they emerge. Water affected plants with a biological control containing parasitic nematodes or use a specific soil insecticide.

Three common pests, all controllable with regular inspection and hand-picking. Slugs and snails (top) graze almost any plant, but leafy hostas are a favourite feast; search for adult vine weevils (middle) in the evening, as they notch the edges of leaves, and water containers with a soil treatment to catch their grubs; lily beetles (bottom) have very specific tastes, and are easily recognized and despatched by hand.

INDEX

Page numbers in *italics* refer to captions to the illustrations